Poetry
FROM THE
Mountaintop

Poetry

FROM THE
Mountaintop

SYLVIA
THORNTON

CREATION HOUSE

POETRY FROM THE MOUNTAINTOP by Sylvia Thornton
Published by Creation House
A Charisma Media Company
600 Rinehart Road
Lake Mary, Florida 32746
www.charismamedia.com

Scripture quotations are from the Amplified Bible. Old Testament copyright
© 1965, 1987 by the Zondervan Corporation. The Amplified New Testament
copyright © 1954, 1958, 1987 by the Lockman Foundation. Used by
permission.

Design Director: Bill Johnson
Cover design by Nancy Panaccione

Visit the author's website: www.sylviamountaintop.com

Library of Congress Cataloging-in-Publication Data: 2011936194
International Standard Book Number: 978-1-61638-686-3
E-book International Standard Book Number: 978-1-61638-687-0

First edition

11 12 13 14 15 — 987654321
Printed in Canada

Dedication

This prophetic book, *Poetry from the Mountaintop*, is
dedicated in honor of my heavenly Father who is the
greatest, most wonderful, marvelous Spirit, who is
deserving of the utmost praise and is credited for being
the Author and Finisher of all things. By His miraculous
power He cultivated the gifts within me by design as His
humble servant to deliver His messages to His people.
This collection of poems speaks to what is on God's
heart and, as a bonus, includes a spiritual encounter
that will inspire, spur you to action, fashion a smile, or
unleash tears of joy when you are touched by His Spirit
through this prose. Each occasion that I met in that
secret place with my heavenly Father and listened to
His soft voice, He deposited and entrusted me with the
essence of His heart for the sole purpose of enlisting
my obedient commitment to share with others as a
declaration in the earth. His select readers must savor
the unexpected, carefully orchestrated journey on the
wings of a poetic awakening by a Father whose free gift
of love is sprinkled in a wonderfully wrapped package
of poetic grace. Hearts will truly be touched and
changed by the saturation of His special anointing. God's
signature kiss and touch is present on each page with the
intent of lasting forever in each heart.

GIVING GLORY TO GOD,

—SYLVIA THORNTON

Table of Contents

Preface

THIS COLLECTION OF poems is a culmination of many precious hours in God's presence over the span of a year. Although this seemed like a long time to me, it wasn't, because God knows best when His work is ready for consumption. The title, *Poetry from the Mountaintop*, and the topics and themes in this book reflect what the Holy Spirit spoke to my spirit. For example, "Mobilize Saints," "Let My People Go!" and "Let There Be Light" are some of the poems that provide a glimpse of what's on God's heart. His desire is to encourage His saints to be charged for action and delivered from passivity. Furthermore, through these poems, God wants to deposit positive words of encouragement into the hearts of His people. The Holy Spirit made me realize that when the onslaught of the enemy comes, I should close the door to despair by praying, praising Him, and letting faith dominate my soul (this brings to my mind the poem titled "Guard Your Heart"). Several of the poems have a connection to the fruits of the Spirit (Galatians 5:22). Admittedly, there are some issues in life that I have struggled with—offense, love, patience, humility, and self-control. But, as the Spirit of God identifies them in you and me, together we can die to our flesh by the Spirit of God burning off ungodly desires through intense fire (like in Daniel 3:26, with the three Hebrew men—Shadrach, Meshach, and Abednego, servants of the Most High God). Know this, the ultimate achievement for us all is the seeking after God's kingdom, personal refinement, holiness, sanctification, and the glorification of God as portrayed in these poems.

My heart's prayer is that you are enlightened by these poems as much as I have been. With God's blessing, it is my pleasure to share with you *Poetry from the Mountaintop*.

May God Grant You Blessings!

—SYLVIA THORNTON

❧ *Mobilize, Saints!* ❧

You are My soldiers on the earth, a battle is waging;

You must fight and stand against the wiles of the devil.

You have dynamite power conceived within you

To be equipped with the prepared truth and ability to firmly
   stand.

My word for the day is mobilize! Saints, mobilize!

Stop the passivity as the enemy steals your hope,

Steals your health, erases your passions, and oppresses your
   mind;

Steals your love and the joy that I so carefully cultivated in you.

You cannot insist on waiting on Me, you are not defeated by
   any means.

My right hand will securely sustain your life.

The power that is within you has been quieted as the enemy
   gains momentum,

Strengthened in his pursuit of those whom he can devour.

Awaken, O sleeper! You have a voice as Abraham and Moses
   had;

I heard their cries, as I'm harkening unto yours.

Speak as one mind and unified member, each with a selected
   gift.

Mobilize—assemble yourselves together to represent My voice
   on the earth.

I need you as you need Me; once again you are My chosen
   people

Created in My own image—we are the same.

Realize the power that has saturated your being

Like a quake ready to erupt, on fire, bubbling over eager to
    escape,

But, yet simmering with a voice extinguished by your own fears.

Trust Me as My strength massages your spirit;

Like a vapor of mist My Spirit inflames every essence of your
    being and My anointing rests on you.

It is not you that created the power; it is you embracing the
    force that quickens your heart

To move mountains and to remove the obstacles smothering
    your life.

Mobilize, saints! Mobilize, saints!

Just don't sit in the pews week after week soaking up words
    spoken in vain;

Your voice is needed throughout the earth.

Before you exited your mother's womb there was a divine plan,

Your purpose was revealed as you bellowed out your first cry;

Let Me hear that same cry when you mobilize.

Be a people of one voice and My arsenal throughout the earth

In every town, region, state, and country.

Summon Me and the banner of victory shall blanket the earth.

Mobilize with prayer and fasting and triumphant faith.

Mobilize and I will lead you in the direction, not by a cloud, but
    by the Spirit of truth stationed within you.

Mobilize! Mobilize, My saints, mobilize! This is God's decree.

A Rainbow Floods Your Heart

A magical rainbow appears displaying splendid beauty

Full of brilliant eye-dazzling colors that we know only God could create.

A thunderous brilliant display of red, yellow, and blue makes a colorful mix in the sky.

So refreshing, Elohim formed glorious wonderment from droplets of rain,

A holy memento proving life's existence is forever shielded from endless waters below.

There is expectancy in the air that the rains and a hint of sun fused, leaving in its aftermath spellbinding delight.

Its existence attracts the attention of unassuming gazers, bathed in their excitement.

This isolated phenomena suspended in the sky seems to neutralize as quickly as each rain shower;

Its blast of brilliance is a temporal monument erected as a symbol of God's mercy.

Everyone hastens to behold this free attraction arched across the firmament;

The cloudy sky is arranged as a backdrop to this awestruck wonder resulting from an honored promise.

This rainbow captures our hearts with the peace it was to bestow as a token of God's providence,

And for a brief moment, it erases all traces of the evidence to each generation of that devastating Flood.

Once again the earth is teetering on the brink of unspeakable sin,

Yet, God so mercifully professed never again would a flesh be cut off by the waters of a flood destroying the earth.

We are graced with the honored rainbow, a spectrum of beauty born out of God's ageless covenant.

❧ Absolute Tranquility ☙

Peace resembling a perfect shore-washed pearl;

Tranquility is craved by all whose rest has vanished.

This is God's coveted fortune that only He bestows upon us,

A constancy that pulsates in the reservoir of our hearts,

An assurance that we abide in the shadow of the Almighty.

Shalom! He is the One who can keep us poised in a state of restful bliss.

We meditate in deserved constant peacefulness;

Alluring peace among saints, an energy that dominates despite the chaos in the earth,

A state of mind easily pardoning us from vexing agitations.

Each of us ponders the grandeur of peace,

A clutter-free mind that is sought after by many and secured by few.

Like warm oil poured on us, quieting the soul,

Peace leaving an enticing stillness and pleasurable calm, a soothing potion penetrating the hearts.

Your mind and body enthroned in complete satisfying rest,

Absent from strife, fear, turmoil and cemented with sacred serenity;

A guarded mind reflective of a renewed heart willing to succumb to desirous tranquility.

❧ *Are You a Change Agent?* ❧

Are you inclined to deposit God's mark in the earth?

The very day you responded to the blessed power of His name

You were purposed with a powerful arsenal—His Spirit took up residence in an empty soul transforming it forever.

You are the evidence of a heart accepting of His love,

Surrendered by the beckoning of His hand to outfit His priestly roll.

We are under the guardianship of the Comforter whose excitement is poised in readying us for our commission.

We cannot escape a personal destiny carefully grafted in our hearts;

We are urged to act swiftly as time lapses with every waking moment.

From the womb, our hearts were secretly rehearsing a change so divine,

Utterly unexplainable, so much so that we search for relief for that longing in our soul

Made complete by the desired intimate knowing of the Almighty.

We are part of the unified body, initiated as priestly agents of change.

In our service to man, we are petitioned for earnest labor to restore depleted souls to righteousness.

There's no detour or excuse for reckless abandonment of our purpose,

A compelling assignment that no one else can execute but you.

Let the words of our mouths and the meditations of our hearts be acceptable to God.

You are endorsed as His special agents packaged with secrets to deliver change in its season.

❧ Bend and Don't Break ☙

Pressures keep coming and pressing in on you to stop you in
your tracks,

Planned to keep you from fulfilling the will of God and realizing
His vision.

Your perfect antidote is right in front of you.

God has His hands outstretched to affectionately grasp yours
between His;

As He brings comfort, He also whispers these words
repeatedly in your ears, "I will not forsake you, I will not
forsake you."

You are His special child, and naturally His face is aglow with
the pride of a doting father.

You are the one grain of sand among billions,

Yet you do not go undetected by God, who sees all.

For His prize child, He has a treasure box to securely place you
in.

Know that you have been raised up to ride the violent storm.

You don't need a boat, you can walk the waters as Peter did;

Keep your eyes fixed on God and you will reach dry land.

Your peaceful escape depends on you—your unwavering faith.

Are you like the house built on sinking sand?

Or bending like a tree limb during the storm?

Each limb that breaks was holding you back from increasing
vigor,

But the limbs that remain can without effort reach the sky.

Your foundation won't break as long as God's words are
immersed in your heart.

And, as you've rehearsed and exercise faith enough times, you
will not break;

Unproductive words can't break you, being laughed at can't break you, and the worst of hurts can only push you closer to your Friend.

Comforted in God's arms, you are under the shadow of His protection.

Break forth in a new song—let your declaration resound a victorious chant that forces the earth to tremble because of its wrongs.

❦ Break Bread ❧

Jesus with His trusted crown is our Bread of Life,

A life that came from heaven and deposited hope in a decaying world.

As our representative, He established the standards to conform to the divine purpose.

The diabolical thief snatched the harmonious presence that was present in the Garden;

Adam and Eve became detached from God because of their joint defiance.

Likened to Eden, God wants us to experience uncensored peace and bliss;

God never purposed for man to be isolated from the glorious ecstasy.

With diligence, let's realign ourselves with complete restoration to God,

Each action should be in conformity to His master blueprint.

He granted us a pardon based on a platform design likened to the prodigal son.

He compels us to break bread on behalf of Him on each memorable occasion;

Do this effortless act to resurrect and honor undeniable sacrifice.

He is our spiritual nourishment; choose Him as your sustenance.

◈ *Create in Me a Clean Heart* ◈

O Lord, we cry, "Create in me a clean heart,"

To secure a heartfelt love that emerges despite the
discouraging responses from others,

A fortitude to command our impulse to abstain from
unfavorable conduct.

Our lives are plagued with failing hopes that, whether we
fathom it or not, position us

To be resilient and self-assured the next occasion an injustice
creeps into the boundaries of our sphere.

None of us is sealed in a vacuum so secure, escaping life's
uncertainties;

They arouse us to the reality that we cannot walk the road
alone,

We are elevated to differing levels by the extraordinary hand
of God.

He places us closer to His bosom and confirms, "Trust in Me,
I'm with you always."

Sustain a pure heart that lets love penetrate unencumbered
within a broken soul.

When we make deposits into the world, we become recipients
of so much more;

In response, our hearts throb with a stanza of righteousness
and love,

And our minds are medicated with the sobering ointment of
peace.

Our hearts quiver with joyous jubilee with a knowing that we
are the workings of His labor.

We honor our Father by letting the words of our mouths and
the meditations of our hearts speak acceptance in His sight.

We capture His grace as it discloses an attitude displayed
through pure hearts.

The ultimate triumph is for us to set our sights on the things
above, which are destined to enrich the world.

❧ *Divine Creations* ❧

We have been selected by the Father of the universe, who is above all and in all,

As servants poised with conformity to His divine will.

We were fashioned in God's own perfection,

Divinely created to fertilize the hearts of men with the good news.

We were introduced to the world to display God's continuous praise;

His bountiful power has been freely bestowed upon us.

We are the special partakers of His incorruptible nature.

God deposited the treasury of His love in the caverns of our hearts.

There is an explicit transfer of God's gift to us—His precious Spirit.

We are vessels made to honor Him with our divine placement,

We have been marked by the Lord as His own.

You are a creation that is fitted to download divine information.

Make no mistake; we are forever aligned with an infusion of power,

Blessed with His provisions like the manna poured out from the sky

With assuredness in Him as the beloved of God,

To wallow in the enlightenment of His marvelous grace;

Blessed as benefactors of priceless provisions imparted to us in anticipation of His marvelous glory.

He opened up Sarai's barren womb to be awakened with divine conception;

Yesterday and today, He promises to be the same.

Like Abraham, you shall inherit a bountiful supply of blessings.

As His divine creation, we're called out of darkness into a
marvelous glory imparted by God.

❧ *Gentle Redeemer* ❧

Gentle like a dove, one so confident in its peace,

Respond to the call—be still and know that He is God.

Welcome the splendor of His natural love

That is freely given to those who dare to embrace it.

You become captivated as He petitions you to come nearer to Him,

A welcome that is as sincere as the mentioning of His name.

Our love must be true in response to what is pleasing to Him;

As we shrink from self we grow bigger inwardly.

Gentle love is like a perfect stanza to a sweet melody,

The power of His engrained love poised in our hearts;

The sweetest aromatic perfume uncovers His essence,

Gives us a keen awareness of the measure of grace and truthfulness in love.

With total surrender, our gentleness becomes completely spontaneous,

As natural as the breath we inhale, coming in sweet succession;

Each breath is a sign that our Redeemer never departs from our midst.

We are free to mimic the gentleness of a lamb,

Our whole dependence is on the Master's rebounding power.

Without hesitation, we can submerge ourselves in the most gentle love of our Redeemer.

❧ God Will Provide That Ram in the Bush ❧

Like for Abraham, the Lord will provide that ram in the bush;

Whether it is in the form of a substituted sacrifice or a morsel
of bread,

Jehovah Jireh will provide all of your needs and much more.

There is little time for fear of Him forsaking you;

His intoxicating love extends to the ends of the earth,

His heart beats fervently for all who belong to Him.

Come to Him and He will shroud your face in His hands.

God moves on behalf of those who are brokenhearted;

His heart aches for the poor, the needy, and those who are
isolated by bars of steel.

He is not a respecter of persons, since all were fashioned by
the same hands.

Yes, He cared enough to provide a cloud by day and fire by
night to show the Israelites their way;

That same love remains today, and as an added bonus, His
Spirit fills our cup.

He will provide the solicited response if you just reach out to
Him.

His desire is a motion for obedience of heart, if you answer the
call.

He opened up Sarai's barren womb to be completed with a
special light to the world,

He arranged the tearing down of the walls of Jericho with the
greatest force;

Today and yesterday, His promises are the same.

A ram in the bush awaits as you dare to call on your Advocate
for help during each test of faith.

❧ God's Love ❧

God's love is the desired medicine and a cure for your pain.

His love is sure to melt away all your cares,

Lavish yourself in His bountiful love.

He often speaks of His mercy, and you may wonder why He has chosen you;

You know you are no different from anyone else.

His love is spread abroad to all hearts who will receive,

His love is far-reaching and recognizable by grace and mercy.

He wants us to emulate His love as we share with others,

God's love prepares empty hearts as they surrender to Him.

Without love there is a far-reaching void that continues to advance.

Man's love is unnatural and most often conditional;

Free yourself completely to experience the depth of God's love.

His nature is so divine, as He is the ultimate source of life.

❧ He Who Lives in You ❧

Faith as small as the grain of a mustard seed grows bountifully.

Having the spirit of faith develops fearlessness each time we
    endure,

We are impregnated with faith dispensed to anchor our souls;

With great expectancy, we have a cord linking us to the
    inspiration of hope.

Faith, hope, and love abide within us as we inch closer to
    sanctification.

We have been given priestly authority to command the earth.

As the Holy Spirit lives in us, we can relish sufficient faith;

Faith is everlasting from generation to generation.

We have the grace and stamina to be tested and perfected by
    fire;

Thus, faith is that spiritual muscle that grows stronger after
    each test.

As we go through, faith exudes as fire deposited in our bosom,
    like a flickering neon sign to remind us that we are not faint
    at heart.

We want to be positioned in the preferred zone of solitary
    peace:

It is the recognition that we are covered by the powerful blood
    and sustaining fire.

We must cradle our assurance in knowing that He who lives in
    us is greater than he that lives in the world.

When you require positive testaments to the confidence in
    God, reflect on Abraham, Moses, Joseph, Enoch, and Noah,
    the righteous heroes of the ageless past.

◈ Humbly We Come Before His Throne ◈

Humbly we come to You, Lord, how else can we position ourselves in Your presence?

You created Your servants, yet You call us friends and priestly children.

O great Majesty, You carefully crafted the universe and the sea below;

As Your created, we are profoundly limited in comparison to Your greatness,

We exist only as we are permitted to serve You.

The full measure of Your love is what You freely dispense to us.

Let's not discredit God with our prideful exhibitions.

To be proud of what? We are servants fused with borrowed power,

Infused with power merely to command this lost and forsaken world;

By grace we gained our salvation and became detached from the world,

Not to think more highly of ourselves than all others.

To remain stable, what a test and measure of His grace.

As we are posed in a position to surrender, we gain boundless influence;

Born as filthy rags and cleansed by Jesus' blood, we reign in spotlessness.

Humility is exhibited by honoring God with noble character.

He paid the price for our sins; our greatest display is to humbly obey His commands,

Shed self to embrace the blending with His Spirit.

He is Creator of all things and Director of the framework of our lives.

As our example, He gave so freely of Himself by graciously washing the feet of His disciples;

Likewise, in solidarity, let's humble ourselves in accordance to His will for us.

Ignite Your Flame

Do you have the passion to celebrate God's sacred existence?

His heart's desire is for us to diligently seek Him.

With full adoration, come to Him all who desire exceedingly more.

That abiding hope to know Him better intensifies into a smoldering flame that is resilient to extinction.

You are a pioneer oozing with liberated strength, purposed to shine like a star in the earth,

Your abundant flame is poised to withstand howling winds of darkness.

We cannot swell the intensity of this flame of our own will.

With the sweet Spirit staged within us, we are bulging with prevailing power;

Joined with God's fire, we remain stable as we tread the darkest valleys,

We resist being ambushed by pitfalls because we are armed with God's powerful arsenal

As we remain encamped by God's flaming sword.

That flickering flame shut up in our bones is finally exposed to the world;

Like the flaming furnace sifting and perfecting, our unwavering efforts are to resist being extinguished.

Together our flames are ablaze with certainty to be dispensed like a consuming volcano in the earth.

❧ *Joy in the Morning* ❧

Joy has a medicinal effect on strengthening the soul.

In the beginning joy and perfect peace were what the enemy stole,

Causing us now to toil with our hands for our life's work.

Don't let the enemy steal your joy; are you going to give him freedom to lurk?

Pillaging our homes causing confusion and chaos; but count it all joy.

When your trust is stayed on Jesus, the enemy has lost power to destroy

The joy that is sparked by a love showered on us from above.

If you allow Him, God will cradle you in His arms and give you peace like a dove.

Meditate on God's Word and put Him first in your life;

Keep peace, joy, and love in your heart and you can turn from strife.

Joy can help overcome any darkness that tries to intrude.

Guard your heart when others hurt you to avoid being rude,

Accept the selfish deed and overshadow it with the peace of a lamb;

You don't want to be so far removed that you miss the Great I AM.

Seize the opportunity to renew your heart and your mind,

Which produces laughter and joy that help you to unwind.

Our dry desert seems so fertile with God's unmerited grace,

In this special oasis lies the richest and most restful place.

Abiding in the shadow of the Almighty is where you should stay;

May "joy in the morning" be your comfort zone as you fast and pray.

✒ Let There Be Light ✒

In the beginning there was light.

That light was ablaze in the universe as the holy Trinity in
oneness declared, "Let there be light";

These solemn words were echoed in unified agreement.

For His creation, God said, "Let there be light," and He blessed
all.

We are positioned in the earth with the same authority to
speak and create light over each measure of our lives.

Under God's authority, speak life under the sanctity of love;

Partnering with God, speak light over the union of families.

Let there be light to weave the hearts of those we encounter,

Let there be light to shine on those who have yet to know Him.

Let your words of declaration ring boldly throughout the earth.

Let there be light over the dark caverns of people's hearts,

Let there be light in every soul to receive the good news,

Let there be light to receive the rich treasury of His glory;

Let there be light generously flowing out of our innermost
being to illuminate the world,

Let there be light in our hearts to break forth like the new
morning;

His Word is a lamp unto our feet and a light unto our path.

We represent the light for the nations and God breathed on it.

Let your light shine before men as an assurance to the world
that Jesus is truth;

Let your light overshadow the darkness in the world, for it is
good.

The brilliance of light is for the world to behold, much like the
gift of the sun, moon, and stars;

Accept His glory and dispense the light within you.

You exhibit great peace, love, and the things of God, and He
called it good.

As life concludes, light shall dominate the earth; God called it
so and blessed it.

❧ Oh, Taste and See That the Lord Is Good ❧

His mercy is the lavished love only a mother can bestow;

Abide in His presence and His peace you will know.

God's love is the nectar from a flower in full bloom,

His kindness is a gift and for more love there's always room.

Let our hearts rejoice in taking Him at His word, He will never lie;

He kept His word with His Son's sacrifice in permitting Him to die.

His regard for us and our well-being is sincere,

He prompts us to obey His commands and it's Him we should revere.

Hear His call for redemption and take refuge in Him,

Surrender yourself in obedience to Him before your eyes grow dim.

And heed His words and the command to love yourselves and others more;

Our spirit waits on the Lord and it's Him we adore.

The Lord looks down from on high over His righteous children again,

When we miss the mark it seems that He forever forgives men.

He's our security, our peace, and our solid rock;

Abide in Him and His secret treasures will be easily unlocked.

He expresses His love and the power of His might,

When we are confronted with oppression we shouldn't hesitate to fight.

Realize that we are never alone or forsaken,

God seems to show up at the opportune time so we won't be shaken.

Oh, taste and see that the Lord is good;

He is our only source, this must be clearly understood.

❧ *In Awe of You* ☙

My God, I look to You and I am in complete awe of You;

None can ever truly measure up to Your greatness.

You are the beacon of light that shines like the brilliance of the sun and moon combined,

Your voice is the sound that echoes like a thousand thunders in the heavens.

Every head should turn with an expectancy of the blending of Your massive strength and tender love.

God, You are glorious, forever to be praised and forever to be revered.

Glory to Your name! We reverence You and our worship is our sweet service to You.

Your gaze is fixed on all of us from above, we are truly special.

In my rest, I can't wait to see Your face and walk in the peaceful garden with You;

You provide consistent contentment the earth has never understood,

I am left breathless by Your dominant love, grace, and mercy.

Your desire is to have union with all of Your people, and Your mercy is offered to all alike.

The mention of Your name is when we are never the same.

In our adoption we reign as citizens, as joint heirs in Your kingdom;

With each breath, we have partaken in your awesomeness and Your glorious splendor.

Praises of His People

Your holy praise is smeared upon our lips.

God is longing to hear the praises of His people;

Hallelujah, we shout and rejoice in our King.

Our Lord reigns, He is everlasting and above the earth, and all power radiates from His hands.

There is more, so much more that He has for His benefactors.

Praise Him and enter into the holy gates,

Shout! He is the King of Glory, Strong and Mighty,

He is the everlasting Father, the Lord over all;

Praise should be steadfastly streaming from our lips.

We were created for praise, He rejoices in His people's wonderfully glorious display,

Our praise is a unified tribute that benefits all the partakers.

Sing, shout, dance, and proclaim the wonder of His love as freely as you know how,

Praise and celebrate Him and declare His greatness.

He hears your praise and it makes Him smile;

Your praise is like the perfect symphony to His ears,

Your quivering lips weep in response to the overwhelming gift you receive.

My Master, my soul is knitted to Yours.

Speak, declare it, and proclaim His magnificence with praise,

Shout Hallelujah—the greatest offering of all to Him.

He urges us to invite Him into our hearts,

Partake of His presence; it begins with praising Him.

Bless the Lord at all times; His praise shall continually be in our mouths,

And we will shout it throughout eternity.

God wants His name proclaimed to the whole world.

✦ *Rejoice in You* ✦

Knowing You more weaves expectancy in the boundaries of my
soul;

Rejoicing in You, I've learned to accept Your proven regard for
me.

You saved me when there was little trace of goodness,

You lavished me with love despite the virtue of my heart being
clouded with discontent.

I greatly rejoice in You, Lord, You are my sufficiency,

You represent my source of peace that replaced spiritual
sightlessness.

There's a rejoicing in my inner self in response to Your glory,

I consistently rejoice in Your incredible favor sprinkled over me
like refined sugar sweetening my soul.

Your voice speaks and I respond to Your oracles;

Your unspoken love presented in the force of Your strength
rejuvenates me.

I rejoice with a jubilant shout, with a song liberated from the
confines of my bosom;

I rest in the depth of You, secure in Your unforgettable caress.

As though for the very first time, I overcome the decoys laid
before me,

I rejoice in a renewed trust as I recognize my absolute haven.

Your outstretched arms await me; I welcome quiet surrender.

I rejoice in Your long-awaited love, my God,

I rejoice with great joy because I've known Your embrace;

With infectious joy, I offer up robust laughter and rejoicing
with a magnitude to make the earth tremble.

✃ Renewed Mind ✃

Invigorate your mind with nothing else but virtuous thinking.

Guard your mind! Those opposing thoughts can inhabit your
     psyche before your eyes finish blinking.

Take no chance in them taking root deep within your mind,

Those poisonous impressions that so often are unkind.

Refocus once more on what you truly desire;

Have the mind of Christ and your heart will ignite on fire.

Sift those fragmented voices and perfect the wrongs you find,

The enemy comes to confuse you and rob you blind.

Be diligent about censoring what intrudes your mind each day,

Do this act to avoid iniquity entering your heart and
     discovering a place to stay.

Safeguard and padlock your heart, and meditate on the affairs
     of your Father;

If you comply, sickness, depression, or selfishness won't be a
     bother.

From the Most High, renew your mind with refined food,

Like a soothing tonic God's peace will bolster a joyous mood.

❧ Shekinah Glory ❧

Holy, holy and majestic You are,

Your power exceeds all that is expected,

Your reigning presence within makes us divine.

We desire more of You, with an overwhelming urgency;

Awaken our souls to Your glorious light and wonder.

Elevated with the oneness with Your intoxicating love
beckoning us closer,

Bolstered with life by Your captivating radiant glory;

Shekinah glory, we offer up praise to Your holy presence.

Hail to the power of the Trinity of our universe.

We bask in Your radiant glory, and we lose ourselves in Your
infinite power,

Releasing ourselves and remaining grafted in Your love.

Love; oh, what love that is uncommonly tasteful to the soul,

Perpetual peace so glorious, so wonderful as an everlasting
sanctuary,

That peace which becomes our resting place as we reside in
Your presence.

We rise to complete ourselves in You, God—Your glory is
awesomely breathtaking.

Shekinah glory is the abiding light and rich heart of God.

❧ That Secret Place ❧

Cherish your inhabitance in the secret place of the Most High;

A sanctuary of perfect peace overshadows a conscience vexed with agitating passions.

In a realm inflated with man's inherent carnal fondness for self-gratification,

Transmit a continence that guards the perfect peace of El Shaddai, and inhale the sweet fragrance of Yahweh or Adonai;

Retain a mind stayed on Jesus, and apprehend His Spirit as a comfort and safe haven,

A mystical place fashioned for an anticipated fusion with God's Spirit.

He unveils His love into hearts longing and striving for the stability of peace;

God's covenant of grace and unmerited favor is nestled in sweet contentment.

We are God's sheep, who expectantly hear His voice and acknowledge Him,

The Lord is the Great Shepherd in whose presence we yearn to be.

As we deposit our shield, and bathe in the anointing of God, He lavishes us in the sweet fragrance of His love,

Therefore, we need not fear evil; we become liberated as we submerge our feet in restful waters,

God hears our voice and delivers us from our enemies and all snares set before us.

We have a connection and reconciliation to our Father,

And we abide in the spaciousness of His comforting arms.

He wants us to know: "Rest, My children, experience the depth of My love."

We can stand with stability and a refined assuredness that He knows our name.

The zealous unity of His people is a flawless melody to God's ears;

He can shoulder our burdens and restore a soundness in our resolve.

Remember, the gifts that He has for us are as free as the nightly presence of the moon and the stars.

We cry holy, He cries holy; "Peace, peace to you, My beloved children."

❧ Let Your Heart Not Be Troubled ☙

Matters of this world make this life seem bleak,

You feel there's no help and your mind and heart grow weak.

Remember, you are not of this world and shouldn't be moved,

God has already won the battle and His strength He proved.

The greatest victory is ours because it has already been won by
God;

He detests evil and rules men with an iron rod.

God promises to save us from all who persecute,

He is Lord and His judgment He shall execute;

Those unholy ones pursue and punish the poor and needy man,

The deceiver, the wretched one, tests your will just because he
thinks he can.

The Lord will repay him for the shameful, harmful acts and
deeds,

There will come a time the wolf and the lamb shall together
feed.

And why not rather let yourselves suffer each wrong.

Fear not, nor be dismayed; be of good courage and remain
strong,

The Lord is your Protector and shields you with a strong
protective wall.

The wickedness of the unruly wicked shall cause them to fall.

These evildoers may boast of having won the battle;

Little do they know, the power of God can make their wretched
bones rattle.

Behold the upright and realize the victorious end for men of
peace.

Hold fast; the folly, the hurts and pains will surely cease.

Let's condition ourselves to trust and take refuge in Him, we need not worry.

Oh, to witness God's mercy, power, and glory, we need not be sorry.

❧ The Essence of Life ❧

Your presence is so glorious and irrational to the natural mind;

Overwhelming joy comes in the morning from Your abounding devotion.

The mammoth strength of Your strong right hand sustains my foes; at the same time, my stature is free to collapse in your tender embrace.

I will forever bask in Your intoxicating love,

Your essence is too marvelous to describe in so few words.

Our image is duplicated by our oneness with You.

With an inward resolve we yield to His Spirit and an unforgettable reward awaits.

His anointing captivates the soul as a new dimension is unveiled;

There is peace and joy presented as a basket full of ripened fruit for life.

Once touched, that person you once knew remains in the distant past;

The newness of what remains is remarkably more than our minds can imagine.

He is the breath and the heartbeat that lures us closer.

The newest love that you have found replaces all that you once thought was splendid.

Extend your hand to be wrapped in His for the remarkable journey,

Breathe a sigh of relief with a knowing that He is forever yours.

Your eyes are opened to see the majestic unraveling of the essence of Him marking you;

You have been transformed with His essence and eternal life.

∞ *The Reflection in the Mirror* ∞

Look in the mirror, God is strategically exposing our tarnished personas.

We bear imperfections close to our breasts as they obstruct the flow of life.

We are exposed to who we have become by our brethren's colorful character.

Who are we to put them on trial because they are the spiritual twins who remind us of our own shortcomings?

Thus, we effortlessly strive and plot to expose the small intricacies in other's lives

Because our own deficiencies are more prominent and in need of restoration.

God is the Lawgiver; He executes righteous judgment of His people.

There is hope as each of us is kissed by God's flickering flame,

We should welcome the active perfecting and our debut as shimmering gold.

The process of refinement requires a precise fraction of time.

As it is for new wine once aged with potency and perfection,

Be assured, at the defined term its bitter taste becomes sweeter and sweeter with each measured day.

To embrace refinement, we are like the moth that lies in a state of rest, emerging transformed with a dramatically altered image.

We must be compelled to reexamine the face in the mirror by peering deep within the recesses of our hearts,

To courageously survey the scars of life that have kidnapped our sweet innocence.

The overdue relief of a wearied prisoner of our own asylum is beckoned to God's throne.

Take heed of the crooked road with the directional signpost urging us to choose life, not death;

We're free to select the alluring journey that we so desire to engage.

Whatever our fancy, the journey doesn't have to end in recklessness; it can align with the masterful plan.

Immerse yourself in God's absolute influence, which positions you as the salt of the earth;

Only then can your reflection in the mirror portray the perfect image of God.

❧ This Mountain Will Be Moved ❧

Lord, build my faith as long and as far-reaching as the rivers
flow.

Many times we fear things, but the reason why we do not
know.

Build my faith, Lord, as far as the mountains encompass the
sky.

In your mind, is the fear as small as a spider or big as a
serpent? Can you explain why?

Whatever it is, our faith will sustain our being.

Can you resist remaining in a constant state of fleeing?

To muster up the strength to endure, we must try.

Face your giants—the greatest fear is that you could die.

Take God at His Word, He will not forsake you;

Stay steadfast and don't grow faint, your faith He will renew.

He will hearken unto your cry in the midnight hour;

Lean on Him, God's strong right hand is His almighty power.

God doesn't have us walk this path alone, His love is pure,

He will take your hand in His and you will be able to endure.

We were not made to be weak or quake in our shoes,

Open your hearts and minds to the good news.

It's through consistent prayer that things can change.

Fear is a spirit; wrap your mind around that—doesn't it seem
strange?

Run the race, keep in step with God and you will always win.

Faith casts out fear, fear keeps us hidden in sin;

Fear cripples, it binds us in overwhelming guilt.

Belief that never wavers is how faith is built.

Jesus died on the cross to set the captives free;

The enemy of your mind wants you to doubt, don't you see?

I hear the Spirit of God saying, "Don't fear, your needs will be
     met.

Stay near to Me and you will have no regret."

He's saying, "Trust Me, trust that My Spirit is always near.

I will not forsake you; respond to My voice, can you hear?"

The only acceptable fear is the fear of the Lord;

Wallowing in fear, God's children can't afford.

God urges us to fear not, be not dismayed.

Arms stretched on that cross, Jesus was not afraid.

The Word says, "Fear no evil, for Thou art with me."

Every mountain will be removed; this should be our decree.

❧ *We Are Conquerors* ☙

The Lord watches and stands guard, interceding on our behalf.

We are called according to His sovereign purpose;

We limit God by the condition of our hearts, by breaching the call.

His ways and thoughts are higher than our thoughts,

Our minds only have the capacity to receive what we allow.

O Lord, awaken us from the deepest slumber,

Make the murky waters of our minds as clear as a crystal prism captured by the sun.

Comprehend God's love as He dispenses hopes and plans in our hearts.

We may never walk the road intended if we don't become conquerors.

If we shrink in faith, insecurities will reside in the recesses of our hearts;

God's purpose will prevail if we allow Him to share our burdens.

Follow His compass, like an invisible rudder that steadies our course.

Let's not resign ourselves to exclusion and infringe on God's divine plan.

We must be persuaded that nothing can separate us from the love that He garnishes upon us.

With God's grace and purposeful presence, we remain steadfast,

We have the stamina to respond to the call with boldness and fortitude;

We are fashioned with a renewed strength by His glorious might and power.

Condition your mind and regulate your heart to be aligned with God;

As you reside in God's presence, He displays His righteous power.

He calms your mind and you cannot help but break your silence to proclaim His glory.

Boldly display your faith; stomp your feet on the trespasser, lift your arms high to represent your victorious stance.

We are conquerors who fulfill our purpose by relying on, adhering to, trusting in Almighty God as we confidently subdue the earth.

Your Brother's Keeper

Our hearts are poured out through honorable conduct.

As we demonstrate uncensored affection for our brother,

We represent the chosen tabernacle of the Lord.

On our behalf, Jesus' pure heart and flawless qualities
abounded in an exhibition of majestic glory.

We sustain salvation and grow nearer to sanctification through
refined hearts;

Our fruitfulness becomes so natural in unwavering kindness.

As our unspoken sacrifices bring a closer connection to God,

We are cloaked with royalty as priests striving for sweet
communion with Him.

We were called out of darkness to shine forth as tenderhearted
people.

As a depository of God's gentle kindness, we become fruitful
servants in the earth;

As strangers to this land, we have been freed by our continued
reverence to God.

The guardian of our souls, He gently beckons us closer to Him.

God has broken the chains off of our hearts to embrace others.

To God be the glory, as He imparts His infinite wisdom in us,

As His command stands throughout the ages, "Beloved, love
one another."

That Song in Your Heart

God will put a new song in your heart.

Arise! Sing to the Lord of joy with endless celebration;

Breed a heart that continues to breathe life into a world
craving solitude.

Oh, such a song brings a warm response despite the condition
of the voice.

A song of grandeur was deposited in your heart by the soft
whisper of His Spirit.

Humbly come to praise Him with gratitude in your hearts,

Pick up the refrain and join in the perfect melody,

A song that diminishes the frailties and murky thoughts that
seems to wander into our minds.

Welcome the sweet chorus of assurance sung in repetition by
the angels on high;

Open your mouth and sing a new song blessed by the
mountains above and seas below.

Have a selection of songs that clap like the rippling waves
against the seashore,

Realizing a song of peace as unique and deserving of urgent
receipt by the world.

What song do you have to be birthed and rehearsed for your
flawless rendition?

Do you have the stamina to sing of peace, joy, or the simplest
verse that captivates the soul?

Be aroused by the somber chorus refreshed like the most
picturesque bouquet,

A fresh song unmatched by the bountiful banquet feast;

Partake in this song as a bonus to your senses and join in the
innumerable company of angels.

❧ *Creator of My Soul* ☙

Beloved of my soul, O Elohim,

My heart overflows with the prevailing love I have for You.

I cannot contain the words that describe your greatness; they are propelled out of my mouth like an unleashed torpedo.

All-powerful, mighty, how glorious and how wonderful You are.

You shaped the vastness of the universe,

You opened up Your heart to welcome each of us with gracious hospitality,

An uncomplicated love so simple and divine covers us in its warmth.

I love You, my Creator, I yearn to know of Your infinite presence.

As a sound from a shimmering brook flowing across the rocks beneath,

The purest water flowing freely as though there is no end to its destination.

Your image reflects back on Your created as we experience transformation under its power.

Let's praise Him, look around to arrest the beauty of His universe,

The voice and hands that took special care and had no rest until that marked day.

O Elohim, the Creator of all things, invites us to participate in His glorious plan.

Your bequeathed love is as absolute as the clearest blue sky and as captivating as the brilliance of the most beautiful rose suspended in full bloom;

Witnessing Your creations forms a smile that was first hesitant to radiate across my face.

You can boast, O Lord; you occupied a barren soul and validated it with vibrant life once again.

After one taste of You, my soul yearns for more captivating exchanges with You.

℘ The Deep Divide Swells Again with Love ℘

You are the guardian of your soul, not charged with the
condemnation of others.

The first thing we are inclined to do is put others on trial for
their wrongs;

We adopt a wounded spirit, and as a safeguard withdraw like a
turtle taking refuge inside its empty shell.

You allowed the enemy to invade unguarded boundaries, in
plotting and birthing a bottomless divide that caused you to
become estranged.

His plot is to lodge a wedge amidst your plans for further
dialogue with one another;

He knows once communication has been silenced, there is little
room for reconciliation.

Your love is poisoned as you engage in blame, and the divide
becomes vast, making room only for more hurt,

Leaving the deepest cavern—designed for two—fashioned for
you to topple into headfirst.

The bruising words are tossed to and fro like an intense tennis
match designed for both of you to lose.

Take a hold of your volatile emotions to fend off the intrusion
of a persistent stronghold.

Your journey began with a basket overflowing with God's fruit,
which you carried skillfully in your grasp;

Then you lost focus and dropped one fruit, then another, until
the contents of your basket was completely depleted.

Helpless, you ponder, How did this happen? How did your
relationship start to unravel?

Wanting to retrace your steps, yet too prideful to embrace the
one resolution;

Have you forgotten the solemn promise you carefully held onto
and the hand you locked within yours with the notion to
never release again?

Your eyes beheld the one you convinced others you wanted to spend every waking moment with; where did that promise go?

That diabolical enemy crept in and stole the passion that united two hearts as one.

God joined you that day, witnessing your convincing vows, and He is still waiting to escort you back to that place of solitude.

The deep divide can revert back to how God designed your relationship to be, becoming one mind, heart, and soul encamped by Him;

The prelude to this love story was to live as spiritual partners for better or for worse.

Reflect back to honor the breathtaking vows you couldn't refrain from being heard by those you held in high esteem.

Please honor the most important guest that day, the One who looked down from above as a doting Father;

He released thunderous applause because marriage is sacred to you, as it is to Him.

That carved-out black hole will be replenished with love, joy, peace, long-suffering, gentleness, goodness, faith, meekness, and temperance;

This is the complete anecdote to a secure union with the one you love.

As you journey to reach that intimate plateau, you are urged to partake in a vigil over your hearts so they swell with love again.

The Expectancy of God

Are you expecting very little in degree to God's love?

Just like the Israelites who saw miracles but lacked confidence to position themselves for their promise,

God's towering abundant grace awaits His latest sojourners.

Do you expect the gift of freedom from life's burdensome conditions?

Do you wait with anticipation for God to meet you before His throne?

Portray a robust appetite and accept what He so freely releases into the reservoir of your heart;

He has life and rich benevolence that can saturate your soul.

Do you expect His tranquil peace to bleed solace into your confused mind?

It behooves you to have a resounding heartbeat that is ignited with soulful passion.

God imagined the world and all that He could supply to grant you special latitude to flourish;

He is the absolute force determined to earnestly pacify your soul.

Renounce an expectancy of lack and hopelessness causing you to pour out nothing at all,

Limited in foresight and silenced by your own sphere of reality.

You are forever pardoned; plan your escape from the prison of your own intellect.

Expect bolstering power to conquer your enemies.

Expect to abound with sufficient blessings.

Expect a renewed heart and mind and a dose of His courage.

Expect peace that melts away all your cares.

Expect grace to flood you with marvelous light.

Expect God to pour out His best for you to experience His long-awaited glory.

Cry aloud, "My hope and expectation are in You, Lord."

Put your hope in God and wait expectantly for His refined love;

God expects your light to shine in response to your call.

❧ The Sustainer of Life ❧

The True Vine gives us life more abundantly,

Our choice of salvation is given completely.

The covenant of agape love is beyond measure,

Afforded to us in God's good pleasure.

The Creator of all things on earth and above,

The Guardian of our souls, His peace like a dove;

His wonderful grace and magnificent power

Sprinkle us with the latter rain shower.

The Light of the world shines ever so bright;

His people bring Yashewah much delight.

His Spirit gives us power, it's not of our own ability;

The act of obedience is the essence of humility,

When we rejoice and praise Him, to God be the glory.

Jesus was the sacrificial Lamb who left us with a great story;

Not just a story, but a life to live by.

Jehovah left the Great Comforter and ascended into the sky.

Praise to our beloved Lord, hail to our Magnificent King!

He is our eternal joy, and our everything.

Our connection in the Spirit and oneness is our Lord.

He binds His sheep together in one accord,

Esteeming the fruits of the Spirit, not the lover of strife;

He is the Almighty God, the only Sustainer of life.

❦ *Virtuous Patience* ❧

Patience is when you stand in a line that seems to grow with
each second passing.

Patience is when you exhibit exhaustive endurance as you
partake in a boundless journey home,

Or when you sacrifice your time and put someone else's needs
above your own—this is patience.

Patience gratifies the Lord, and it profits the soul.

If we permit our hearts to be engrafted in Christ, patience can
become an enticing handiwork.

As any other endowment, patience glorifies the Lord.

By grace we fulfill our longed passion to overcome life's
encumbrances;

It curtails bruised feelings and strengthens uprightness in spirit.

Grow accustomed to conditioning your heart to be unsparing in
the acceptance of others,

Which proves to our Father that His people are truly following
His own heart.

We can accomplish reformed conduct with the spiritual
realignment of our minds as we seek patience.

God's love is amplified with the emphatic announcement of a
heart surrendered to Him;

It's accomplished by the wholesome goodness that is imparted
through us to others.

It's been simply said—patience is a virtue!

Virtuous, as its outpouring becomes manifested through the
unchanging proclamation of love.

❧ Your Cup Runneth Over ❧

Merciful and Holy You are.

Your head is anointed with oil and your cup runneth over

As tranquil peace constitutes its restful state.

Make goodness and mercy your recipe for love,

As it ripens like bunches of grapes within your soul, plentiful
and flooded with an intoxicating elixir.

Like the sparkling crystal exploding in beauty once touched by
the flaring rays of the sun,

You will engage your breakthrough as a sojourner of truth,

Beckoning each heart into perfect oneness with God's;

An affair of the heart unrecognizable by those unpretentious
ones.

The sweet flavor of unselfishness received with welcomed bliss,

Love born with intensity, bursting with power to influence;

A love torpedoed into open hearts primed to receive,

Exposed like a notch on a tree forever marked with distinction.

Love is less of a novelty to the compassionate soul; it always
upholds its newness,

Your cup shall overflow with goodness and mercy all your days.

As you embrace the cup, drink from its living waters; the
rewards are forever.

❧ Speak, Lord, Your Servant Hears ❧

I hear Your voice in the sounds of the doves in the cool
   morning air.

I hear Your voice in the laughter of the children bringing life to
   the playground.

I hear Your voice in the whistling train echoing in the distance.

Yet, I hear Your voice cry out when the children's bellies
   grumble in union from nagging hunger;

I hear Your voice when the homeless man's cardboard box is
   beaten down by the icy rain.

I hear Your voice when a mother pleads for mercy over the
   gunshots in her neighborhood.

I hear Your groanings when the color of one's skin paralyzes
   man's hearts with hatred.

I hear Your still small voice that urges us to pray;

I hear Your still small voice that brings peace and joy to a
   quaking heart,

Your voice that seems to diminish our pain like melting wax;

Your voice that is a strong and mighty force;

Your voice that reveals the wonders of Your faithful love;

The voice that hides us in the shelter of Your presence;

The voice that lavishes us with Your goodness;

The voice that directs us to be strong and courageous.

For You are our hiding place, Your voice is what we long to
   hear.

"O Israel," He said, "Oh, my people, listen as I speak."

The Lord hears His people when they call to Him for help;

Speak, Lord, Your servant hears.

Speak, O Lord, Your servant hears; speak, Lord.

A New Attitude

We must have the same attitude that Christ had;

He didn't complain or fret, He was forever glad.

You have problems you can't handle? He can give you rest.

This cultivated peace is not of your own doing, it is God's best.

Start rejoicing and let your heart be clothed with peace;

God's glory and anointing, He will surely release.

You may feel weak, but He supplies the strength to endure

Whatever you are going through; you will have victory for sure.

Rejoice and be glad, it is a new year, a new day.

You are wrapped in God's loving arms, when you pray.

If you are lost, lean on the Comforter, He will make you strong;

Ask the Holy Spirit to fashion you with a new attitude and you
   can't go wrong.

Like shedding of old skin, let your burdens fall to the ground;

It's the gentle peace of God, which you have found,

His powerful glory changes you into His likeness.

Selfishness, self-pity, malice, jealousy, envy—stop all that
   mess!

With a new character, you're no longer driven by strife;

Live out the goodness that has been planned for your life.

Joy to the world, the Lord has come;

It's a new year, a new day that is bound to affect some.

He came to electrify your hearts with His divine love.

Looking from on high, He's sitting on the right, far, far above.

We can never succeed by our own will or own might;

Walk with a new attitude, it's not your fight.

Boldly proclaim: "I can do all things through Christ who strengthens me!"

Don't get sidetracked; you'll be alright, you will see.

Having a new attitude to act right, to talk right, and to walk right,

You can climb higher and higher like a soaring kite.

It's a new attitude; it's a new you!

Be Still and Know That I Am God

The Lord is our salvation and illuminated light;

In God, His Spirit and Son, we should delight.

We are complete with a oneness with the Savior, He's our rest;

We shall release His love because He expects our best.

Taste, oh, taste and see that our God is good,

Coming before His throne, where many righteous have stood.

You too can make your way to the throne of grace;

Whatever you've done, there's never lasting disgrace.

Put your mind at ease, free of contempt, guilt, and shame,

Forgiving your sins and depositing peace in your soul is God's
aim.

Dwell in God's secret place on high and make it your refuge,

You'll find that no problem or care is too daunting or huge.

It is He who is the Judge and He who holds the rod.

Be still and know He is Almighty God,

His mighty right hand will smite your foes;

God has ears to hear and eyes to see, He always knows.

Your life may seem fragile but it's in His hands.

Follow Him and receive His love commands.

The Spirit of God that dwells within us is our source and guide;

God will shield us and in His shadow we can abide.

Yes, we can willingly choose God and freely trust.

Let's refrain from evil and be delivered, God is just.

Snares of the world and weaknesses that we've overcome,

We are the anointed ones, and more priestly we have become.

Preserve your faith and acknowledge that God's kingdom is
real,

And know the enemy comes to kill, destroy, and steal.

Be still, you don't have to fret, peace is your treasure;

And appreciate all the faith that God gives you in full measure.

❧ Bring Glory to Your Body ❧

To you, your body may seem like an empty outer shell

Many times overlooked and shamefully neglected,

A sacred body tattooed, scarred, pierced, and deformed; the
home where the Spirit is to reside.

You must not feed the temple ungodly things; honor and glorify
this special monument.

It's not a simple concept for our natural minds to grasp; marvel
at the closeness to God's Spirit.

Aren't you inclined to keep the temple swept clean of clutter?

Maintain stability and strength to avoid the shattered residue
of the world.

Of worry, hatred, greed, pride, and self-gratification, all that
attacks and erodes the flow of life.

You are the innkeeper who must be selective of what enters in.

Keep the inner and outer walls clear of frequent staining and
soiling,

Be a suitable steward over the one thing God has freely given
you charge over.

Minimize your weaknesses and bring your body into subjection
to God's will,

Don't succumb to every whim that is dedicated to overtaking
your mind.

Adorn your temple with acceptable clothing to avoid attracting
unwelcome attention;

Clad in spiritual holiness, your body will receive the glory of
God as it shines through and becomes an attraction for
others.

Like a neon sign beckoning others to partake in God's
magnificent splendor,

Present your bodies as a living sacrifice to bring glory to God.

❧ *Contain Your Emotions* ❧

We were fashioned with uncontained thoughts and emotions.

With so many feelings burdening our minds and blocking the character of God,

They can intrude on the flow of life and our destined union with God's Spirit.

We have to cultivate our minds and hearts so they can be free of emotional ties.

The compartments of our minds are lined with dust bunnies of life which swirl around to and fro by the slightest wisp of air;

They are distracting, unsightly, and not easily controlled.

We have to sweep up the filth and acknowledge the uncleanness.

But, no one can clean our house for us,

You can't hire a maid to take care of the disarray.

Are you harboring ill will towards another because your heart is hardened like stone?

We must acknowledge our emotional baggage by letting the Holy Spirit reveal it to us;

He will help you examine the reason for the messes in the first place.

Has pride crept in and kept you from realizing who you have become?

Have you received discernment from the One who saves?

Let's be sensitive to the misplaced emotions that hinder our spiritual walk.

Shelter your peace, don't be blinded by the short-circuited emotions.

You must not shoulder your burdens alone; your emotions can be arrested to bring you back into conformity with the mind of Christ.

❦ Dance Like David ❧

God has choreographed a special rhythmic waltz chosen just
for you,

A lovely stanza so your feet can master the smooth cadence.

Remember your uniqueness blossomed from a specially
fashioned workmanship.

He encourages you to embrace the first step, to accept His
invitation to have a moment of oneness with Him.

Dance with Him in the midnight hour where no one else judges
your missteps,

Knowing that others will accept nothing other than a flawless
rendition.

Only God will glide you back to the artful steps, causing your
bewilderment by His perfection.

Like no other, God is patient and gracious as you seek
forgiveness for continually stepping on His toes.

You stop to ponder the special song chosen only for your ears.

His heart of compassion is so encouraging and His deliberate
guidance so reassuring to make you respond confidently to
His will,

Knowing you can master the two-step, the cha-cha, and the
tango in which your cheek rests on His.

God's love is in every song and His grace is linked to each
dance with you.

You won't be alone clutching the wall in fear of dancing alone;

With your hands clutched in His, He communes with you as
you dance away life's cares.

Like David, you can dance and dance before the Lord.

Do you accept the invitation to freely dance with Him?

You will never be alone again as you've chosen to steady your
eyes on God's as the two of you dance in perfect precision.

❧ *Do Offenses Penetrate Your Armor?* ❧

Don't let offenses creep in because someone didn't acknowledge your presence.

You take offense because words spoken in vain seemed disrespectful.

Being offended is a selfish emotion indicating it's really about you and only you;

It's saying, I am so important, how dare you say this or do that to me?

But contrary to the world, God sees you as priestly, and royalty has impeccable manners.

Show grace and character that is like Jesus.

Idle words are just empty puffs of air; don't let them be a stumbling block.

If you have self-control and are clad in your armor, cruel words can't penetrate.

You are determined to stand tall, and love can deflect vile words and ill deeds.

Are you going to carry around someone else's baggage for days, months, or even years?

The onslaught of offenses trespassing in our minds keeps us trapped and bound like chains wrapped around our necks;

You become connected to that offender who has moved past the offense, or may not know how the words were perceived.

When that spirit of offense pulls at your heart, don't invite him in; shut the door in his face.

Many times Jesus could have been offended, yet He resisted the temptation because love casts out fear.

Recognize who you are; certainly the true offender has assessed who you are down to your stability and valor.

Look in the mirror at the armor shining back at you reflecting strength and the badge of a light bearer.

Don't keep opening the wrong doors; release the offenses and make room for forgiveness to erase all wrongs.

ॐ Empty Your Soul to Me ॐ

God asks that you call on Him; He is awaiting your surrender.

He says, "I sense your heaviness, release the weight into My hands.

You can't carry the burden alone; enter into my sanctuary.

You want to stand tall and claim the cares of the world as your own.

I made you to look to Me as your source and there is no weakness in that.

I am the friend who towers over you from on high,

My great right hand will lift you out from your troubles.

The crushing weight of the world is smothering your hopes,

Your thoughts meditate on the many things that are causing your mind to drift;

Your are so immersed in your sorrow you can't even cry.

That black hole keeps sucking you further into isolated darkness."

"I am here," He says, "My voice is crying out to you.

Release your troubles to Me, I have won every battle before;

Remember Jericho, remember Job, be reminded of the Israelites and their promised journey home.

In My help, I showed up in the fire by night and cloud by day and My presence remains infinite;

Welcome peace that spreads like a white vapor throughout your soul.

Extend your cup and I will fill it to the brim with a joy that will sustain you;

My spirit is quickened in you to let you know you can shift your burdens to Me."

◑ *Gentle Breeze* ◐

The Spirit of God is the whispering gentle breeze, yet so
explosive with the power to command change.

I have met Him when I took the guard off my heart and finally
surrendered myself to Him.

When I truly trusted, I had no misgivings; I knew that He was
as real and extraordinary as the sun and moon, in which He
formed

A passionate spirit within my soul with a special connection to
mine...if I just choose to let go.

For so long I barely managed to do what I naturally know how
to do best,

Attempting to run a life which is not my own, struggling like a
newborn fledgling bird overwhelmed with frustration as it
struggles to take flight;

As I fail miserably, I realize I have a source who knows better
than I what I need pertaining to my desires.

My mind and will must be free to receive what my God has
artfully planned and destined for me,

A life of security and pleasure in a secret place where only a
few hold the key to enter in,

His throne, leading to His arms, where His presence captivates
my attention.

The essence and heart of God encourage me to experience
oneness with Him;

I know His caress, I sense His soft touch on my head, and I
welcome the spiritual waters that flow like a river from the
crown of my head to the soles of my feet.

Who is the one Spirit who provides the peace that God
bequeathed to you?

He is my friend, my confidant and guide when none other
knows the place I am in, when darkness tries to overshadow
my peace.

We have heard of peace like a dove, a state of being that we
long for, a love that never fades.

His Spirit releases an unfamiliar blending with the same sweet
nectar that can be lavished on others,

A Spirit that is available to all who accept His fortune and
invitation to receive in abundance,

An offer to abide in His presence forever as the spark ignites
into a burning fire within.

Holy Spirit, you establish a newness within me, as your gentle
breeze sweeps across my face.

❧ *God So Loved the World* ❧

Love is the heart and essence of God,

A state of being realized by the fusion of spirits and the defiance of one's own selfish will.

God's Spirit spoke and continues to speak, "Love covers a multitude of sins."

In truth, this perfect spiritual fruit can arouse you to treasure even the most disregarded soul.

God can open your eyes to extract the beauty beneath people's flawed characters that have deteriorated from years of rejection;

One kind word or a glance plastered with a smile can alter a life forever.

Only when our conduct is controlled by the Spirit of God can we sustain pure love.

A steadfast love becomes eternal, and can forgive and release hatred and ill deeds from another.

In demonstration of grace, God so loved the world that He gave His only begotten Son.

The simplest gift to another is to be knitted together by a pure heart;

As we walk by the Spirit, our heart swells with forgiveness and discards all offense.

God's complete love and supreme image is a blueprint of what our character should embody.

Or ponder the simplest touch of a mother which can shape her innocent one's shameless existence.

Bearing one another's burdens allows us to freely supply the one thing our own lives may be lacking;

Like a potent medicine, love heals wounded hearts screaming for relief.

When you experience the true depth of God's love, it is like a boomerang that is released freely, yet knows how to make its way back from whence it came.

Love is like the dew that softly canvasses a grassy hill, making a marked impression as it glistens in the sun as if to say, "Feast on my beauty."

Love is as gentle as the first drops of rain that seem to have the perfect timing to become relinquished into the earth.

As love incubates and ripens within each of us, it unveils God's secrets.

As we choose love, the pendulum for eternity balances on one promise: that God so loved the world.

❧ *God's Agent* ❧

A demeanor so joyful, as though every day was sunny;

She released her love like perfectly sweet honey.

There are few who I've known with such grace and style;

I regret that I knew her for such a short while.

But...that short time was marked with such caring eyes

And words that I considered very, very wise.

Yet, not my mother, but a dear substitute.

With her quiet deeds she bore great fruit.

If I were to judge, fruits of the Spirit bore her soul—love, joy, and humility.

She never once complained, despite her lack of agility.

I loved her as a dear friend and I wasn't the only one.

She ran God's race well until her job was done.

As I knew her, there was never a contrary spirit or ill deed.

With her sincere devotion to God, she took the lead;

In prayer, she would say to me, "I surround you with faith and love."

The one comfort I have is she will rest in precious arms in the sky above.

To do a kind deed for another she wouldn't think twice;

Everything had to be her best, nothing less would suffice.

It seemed as though she watched over each of us like a mother hen tending her nest;

This dear matriarch spread her love around, she was the best.

My only regret is that I never got to say good-bye,

But she knew the spiritual connection neither of us could deny.

A beautiful soul, a dear friend who was always true,

I love you, my dear friend; this tribute is for you.

❧ Guard Your Heart ❧

God examines the condition of a man's heart.

Fasten your heart securely under lock and key

To avoid the onslaught of snares and darts directed towards
your mind and heart

Intended to get you off course, derail your purpose, and keep
you from your assignment.

Guard your heart against vain words and deceitful lies,

Barricade your mind against words that take root and hijack
your heart,

Causing you to meditate on things that are not profitable to
the soul.

Your heart is pliable like clay, easily overtaken by harboring
deep wounds unless washed by the cleansing blood.

Our purpose is to serve God with all of our being and love Him
with our whole heart;

How can broken hearts seek and yearn for God unless they
praise Him with whole hearts fixed and steadfast?

I ask you, how can our hearts be draped with the mantle of
peace and blameless integrity?

God cautions us to keep our hearts with vigilance and let not
our hearts be troubled because there is always hope;

Our Father will intercept our prayers and respond to our needs.

We are made complete by the words of our mouths and the
meditations of our hearts being acceptable in God's sight.

Endorse the precepts of God and hold them nearer to your
closely guarded heart.

❧ *How Big Is Your Flame?* ❧

Do you hold a passion to connect with God's sacred existence?

His heart's desire is for us to diligently seek Him.

With adoration come to Him, all who desire exceedingly more

With a flicker of hope to know Him better; it flourishes into a smoldering flame that resists fading,

It will not extinguish even with the strongest gust of wind or an unexpected shower.

You were fashioned with a purpose to shine like a star in the earth;

Your bold flame is hot enough to steady the howling voices of darkness.

We cannot swell the intensity of this flame of our own will.

With the sweet Spirit within us staged with a purpose, there is an expectancy to bulge with surging power.

With God's fire, we can stand up to the challenges of this world;

Refuse to let circumstances shrink you and smother your flame, reducing your hope to ashes.

As you remain encircled in God's flaming sword, there is liberty.

An internal flickering flame that was once shut up in your bones is finally exposed to the world

Like the eternal furnace that keeps perfecting, purifying, and changing; your flame can only be extinguished with your denial and shameful pride.

❧ Infallible Recognition Comes from God ❧

You're exhausted waiting for others to acknowledge all that you
have done;

You recognize this is not the most modest race that you have
been chosen to run.

Look to God, man is not qualified to grant you all that he
knows to confess.

You encourage people's flattery hoping it will help you escape
from your distress.

You cannot require others to validate who you are;

In God's eyes you are like a bright star,

Release all of the things of the world that you desire because
they are not meant to last;

Align yourself with His will and leave your inflated ego in the
past.

Desiring recognition is part of the blinding sin that pivots you
further away from God's glory.

Refrain from distorting His promises, let your mind reaffirm the
story.

"The only approval you should seek is Mine," is what the Lord
would say;

You hear His voice but disregard His words, to His dismay.

What you have for the world is not for your own pleasure,

It is liberating to ponder the things from above purely for good
measure.

Don't stray from the weaving of your heart to God's, which
pulsates with wholesome grace;

His unmerited favor transcends any mortal man's mockery and
smiley face.

Let's not heed man's failing plan and spend time in worry.

When you seek man's approval, remind yourself of Jesus'
example—His only motive was to bring His Father glory.

Jesus Is Lord

The world wonders who I am;

This is truth—I am the great I AM.

I marched deliberately to the cross for you.

Then why am I so obscure in your minds?

I made My illuminating light available to the world.

I walked the earth as a servant and a prototype for you to imitate.

I flooded you with My love, despite the painful rejection I received.

You have a choice to believe in the wonder of My love;

Without a price I give and freely you can receive.

I asked My children to come to Me when they are burdened.

God's Spirit who is in you recognizes who I am;

Don't let the enemy ambush and cloud your thoughts.

I was born of a virgin, a great, magnificent, undefiled birth breathed of God.

God's perfecting of Me caused My acts to replicate spotlessness.

In the beginning the Word was God, and sin brought shameful dishonor to His name;

God tried endless times to erase the wrongs, but man's hearts remained defiled.

Don't doubt who I am, I am in you and you in Me.

You were acquainted with Me by a foreshadowing truth,

And sealed securely by My promise.

You are born out of love and chosen by the Holy Redeemer

To be united forever by the confession of My name.

Countless will fail to understand My purpose on the earth,

Numerous will stumble because of a scarcity of knowledge.

Many will have hearts that are waxed cold;

The enemy is waiting for My people to refuse to recognize Me.

I am the one and only risen King of Glory, who was and is to come;

Worship Me and through Me to approach the holy throne of grace.

My love is poured out to the world as probable cause to accept Me, if you will.

Surely, I will come and you will know I am the Bread of Life,

The living sacrifice who has risen and advocates for you.

Every knee shall bow and every tongue confess, Jesus Christ is Lord.

Jesus, you may call Me, Yeshua, Emmanuel, The Great I Am, The Holy One, Prince of Peace, King of Kings, Dayspring, Root of David; whichever name soothes your soul,

But know this: I am your Lord, the Messiah who was sent to redeem the world.

Know Who You Are

You are the likeness of Christ, therefore be confident in whom you portray.

You are as precious as the stars and the moon that were fashioned for your pleasure,

One akin to the most priceless jewel ever discovered in the recesses of the earth

That with years of being grasped in the earth's bosom emerges at the appointed time;

As a rare stone sculptured by the loving hands of God, likewise we were fashioned by those same hands.

The same God who took precious time to know each hair on your head,

He carefully chose the color of your eyes and the formation of the temple in which His Spirit resides.

Know that you are so splendidly made that only a distinct fingerprint unmasks your true identity.

With His love, He unveiled a distinct carbon copy of Himself and He has armed you with the power to influence;

It is you that He has chosen to influence the earth with His virtue,

It is you that has been sharpened to be the moral agent.

You are no longer a spectator; take your place as one destined for a sacred appointment,

As His saints emerge together they claim a residue of hope to free the earth.

His Holy Spirit first breathed the air that you now borrow.

God formed you with every intention of being His vessel of honor,

Honor Him by knowing who you are as His mighty agent launched as a light bearer.

Let My People Go!

The enemy of your mind has succeeded in restraining you

With efforts to keep you in shackles and enslaved to the world.

Just as He demanded in Egypt, "Let My people go,"

Again, God is saying, "This is the time that my people are released to speak My words into the earth.

Be released from the paralyzing fears.

My people must realize the power that flows within them must come forth.

You are in Me and I in you." What explosive power!

This is the day to spring forth like a jack-in-the-box as though freed for the very first time,

That, once touched, leaps as though it has boundless power and might.

Have no fear and no restraints; reject false words, make them cry in vain.

Refrain from the complacency and the reckless neglect.

You are positioned to be a part of the unified body of saints in the earth.

It is not you doing the works; you were adopted to become God's mouthpiece,

Whatever you decree in faith or do in His name shall come to pass.

You are filled with the good news and able to make followers of Christ.

God demands that the enemy let His people go; "They will secure the lands as My ambassadors.

Be still and know that I am God and witness the deliverance of the lost.

Drink from My well of sweet waters," is His welcoming invitation.

Awake, O sleeper, God's Spirit has sounded the trumpet for
His people to respond to the call;

Don't be deceived by the seducer of humanity, he must let
God's people go.

As the Moses of today, let your mind be energized to carry the
torch for freedom;

Follow God's instructions as He equips you to fulfill His desire,
for you to release yourself to Him.

❧ Never Forsaken ❧

You know I am with you when my soft whisper awakens you to
a fresh new day.

That was I, your Creator, as you prayed and showed interest in
knowing My voice;

My acknowledgement was in the comforting words spoken to
you in the midday hour.

You must know that I will not forsake such a friend.

As My sheep who, at times, wanders aimlessly through life,

I am at your disposal to redirect your path.

My regard for you goes beyond simple words; it's like the
lasting kiss that I placed on your cheek.

It's the unspoken words that resonate My love,

And it is My invisible presence that holds the key to silencing
that longing for a satisfied soul.

The single touch of the Almighty gives you the fullness of life,

The power of My love is the lifeline to an injured heart.

Taste the sweetness that is purer than anything the world could
ever offer;

Enjoy complete communion and a lasting partnership as
partakers with Christ.

God's powerful hand is positioned to silence your foes and to
break yokes,

The gift of His Spirit is the peace that can evaporate all
uneasiness in an unsettled heart.

God is omnipresent and His vastness is a reassurance that you
will never be forsaken or walk alone.

❧ *Outstretched Arms* ☙

With my unwavering love, I died for the world

For you to experience My love and see My glory.

I could not deny My Father's glory, so I felt honored to wear that painful crown.

I had a promise to fulfill for the coming age;

As the living sacrifice My death was made easy.

I thought of you, My sons and daughters, not of My own desires.

Like any man, I felt the pain, but I relied on my Father's love that was poured out upon Me as it is being poured upon you.

I would do it all over again so the world could witness the triumph of God.

The love I have will never fade and My peace will last throughout eternity.

I ask that you follow My example in your compassion for service;

Don't forsake others for yourselves, pour out an unselfish love that I have deposited in you.

The mask of deception is fading; you and I are one, one in spirit.

You are a perfect imprint of the Son; take your sword and follow Me.

You are the voice that will convince others that My love and Spirit abide in all,

Stretch your arms wide to serve the world.

Like Moses and the tablets, I have given you words that are printed on your hearts.

Touch the world in an unselfish way as I had done before I departed.

When you have done your best, My embrace welcomes you;

My arms will be outstretched to greet you, My good and faithful servant.

⊗ Proclamation of Praise ⊗

People, come with rejoicing and whole-hearted praise;

Proclaim your thankfulness with a thunderous clap offering,

Let your feet lead with a contagious dance movement.

Form an enthusiastic assembly, bonding with the angels in their
hallelujah chorus;

Welcome deserved contentment knowing you deposited
ornamental praise in the heavenlies.

We know fully God's expectancy of limitless praise, worship,
and thanksgiving.

Worship the Lord in the beauty of holiness and rejoice in God's
majesty and glory.

Celebrate His grandeur; present Him with the beautifully
unwrapped gift He so deserves.

Your lips clamor to make bountiful melodies that can't wait to
erupt in the earth.

God receives you at the window of His heart to fuse your spirit
with His.

Honor your beloved with sacrifice, rejoice and lavish Him with
uninterrupted love.

The splendor of your voice has been conditioned and staged
with high praise from your lips,

A holy chorus richly rejoicing in reverent communion with God.

Praise the Lord, jubilantly rejoice in Him until there is an
explosion of His glory;

Exuberant, exalted, exhorted, earnest praise, a celebration of
His holiness.

Give to the Lord the glory due to His name; lay prostrate and
be forever in awe of Him.

A Body Addicted to Self-Control

As funny as it may seem, how about an addiction to
self-control?

Let your mind and body refrain from a will of its own, choosing
from a smorgasbord of cravings;

You must be subject to the spiritual desires waging war on your
invasive appetites.

We should strive for a disciplined mind.

As we exercise knowledge, we develop self-control.

Every addiction stems from boundless appetites

For the things of the world, with overwhelming cravings for
artificial sensation;

We become idolaters of stimuli that hijack our sense of
reasoning.

We must arrest our strong urges and lavish hunger.

The negative influences are like a yoke around our necks.

Counteract this thirst with righteousness that explodes in the
chambers of your heart;

Do not yield your body as an instrument of wicked cravings.

We can't become complacent and allow our members to
dominate our souls.

Let no sin rule as an idol in your mortal, perishable body.

We can have an overflow of God's full anointing and mercy and
grace.

Make the Holy Spirit content that His home resides in you,

Don't grieve the Spirit by defiling His temple.

Welcome the Holy Spirit to reside in a mansion that is adorned
with cleanliness and purity;

Let yourself be controlled by the Holy Spirit's fruitful service,

With ease you can sustain holiness in mind, body, and soul.

Present your body as a living sacrifice holy and pleasing to God.

If My People Would Humble Themselves

Humbly we come to you Lord, how else can we be?

O Majesty! You carefully crafted the universe and the sea below;

We are small in comparison to Your greatness.

We exist only as we are permitted to serve others.

The full measure of Your love is what You freely give.

Let's not discredit You by exhibiting proud and boastful expressions,

We cannot afford to repeat the terrible injustice caused by that first sin.

We have power to command this forsaken world, but are too weak to ignite our flame.

Can you think more highly of yourself than someone else?

What a test and measure of Your devoted love!

As we have surrendered, we gain boundless faith.

Humility exhibits itself by honoring God with hearts that resemble His.

He is the source of our strength and our mere existence;

He paid the price for our sins, therefore the most beautiful service is to humble ourselves,

Disregard self and become consumed with the needs of others.

Our Creator, the director of the framework of our lives, esteems humility.

Teresa Carter

~~teresa~~
teresa @spcbuffalo.org

embrauza @gmail.com
Elizabeth Brauza-Holmes

come to have first place in everything. For in him all
through him God was pleased to reconcile to himself
making peace through the blood of his cross.

The Holy Gospel   *Luke 23:33-43*
When they came to the place that is called The Skull,
on his right and one on his left. Then Jesus said, "Fatl
are doing." And they cast lots to divide his clothing. T
but the leaders scoffed at him, saying, "He saved othe
God, his chosen one!" The soldiers also mocked him,
saying, "If you are the King of the Jews, save yoursel
is the King of the Jews." One of the criminals who we
"Are you not the Messiah? Save yourself and us!" Bu
God, since you are under the same sentence of conder
justly, for we are getting what we deserve for our dee
he said, "Jesus, remember me when you come into yo
you will be with me in Paradise."

❧ Take the Limits Off of God ☙

God is pleading with us to take all limits off of Him.

He created the heavens and the earth, can't He do all else?

How can we doubt what He can do and has already done?

We alone have contained ourselves and limited God;

Expect the miraculous power of God to change your flesh-driven thoughts.

God will not be mocked by our failing faith.

Without limits, the anointing can raise you to do things beyond your imagination,

Miraculous things that mere men cannot fathom completing. Staying humble is the prerequisite to His limitless power.

Take the limits off of God and be free in Him;

It's your mind and intellect that prevent you from experiencing the vastness of God's Spirit.

When we work in unison with Him, our power is limitless.

We need to shed the doubt and fears and receive all that God has for us;

We must be free to be who He called us to be and exhibit His greatness;

We need to cease from short-circuiting God's overflowing power.

Let go and let God have His way in you.

❧ Seek My Face ❧

If God's people who are called by His name will humble
themselves, pray, and seek His face, and turn from their
wicked ways, they will hear from Him.

If we crave after unfulfilling promises on earth, we miss out on
the true treasures from on high.

God makes Himself available to each of us, and our passion
should be to pursue Him with our whole heart.

The world's plan is for us to become preoccupied with life's
worries and events so that we forget about all else.

Don't let your moral conduct be jaded, causing you to become
estranged from God;

Refrain from all forms of impurity that your untamed desires
may suggest.

Seek Him in the midnight hour or when you are basking in the
noonday sun; no matter when, you will find Him.

God desires a heartfelt search to know Him more, to know His
voice and respond to His love.

Once you connect with Him, His voice is recognizable forever;
claim Him as your Source and Maker of everything.

Seeking Him starts with a tugging at a heart that seems it
could never be satisfied,

Until that day that you knock at His door and are able to enter
freely into His presence.

After continued communing with Him, the things of this world
become insignificant and you become changed forever.

Seek after what is true and perfect and you will be empowered
with a special union.

Be an imitator of Jesus, follow His examples in your endless
pursuit of holiness;

Your search for Him is a free admission into a presence so
divine.

About the Author

SYLVIA THORNTON WAS writing poetry for leisure at a young age, but just recently God inspired her to write prophetic poetry. She grew up in a Christian home and had parents who tried to honor God's Word and welcomed His Spirit into their home. Sylvia was born in Kentucky, and was among eleven children raised in Wisconsin. Sylvia resides in Madison, Wisconsin with her husband, Malcolm. She has two grown children whom she is proud to say honor God with their love and attention. Sylvia has a heart for people and she knows her destiny is to spread God's word to the nations.

Contact the Author

Sylvia Thornton
P.O. Box 711
Madison, WI 53701-0711
608/335-5762
Email: info@sylviamountaintop.com